SEVEN WORDS
TO THE CROSS

*The Seven Last Words and
The Art of Understanding
Difficult People*

FULTON J. SHEEN

Bishop Sheen Today
280 John Street
Midland, Ontario, Canada
L4R 2J5

www.bishopsheentoday.com

Library of Congress Cataloging-in-Publication Data

Names: Sheen, Fulton J. (Fulton John), 1895-1979, author. | Smith, Allan J., editor

Sheen, Fulton J. (Fulton John), 1895-1979. Seven Words to the Cross. - Registered in the name of P.J. Kenedy & Sons, under Library of Congress catalog card number: A180603 following publication May 5, 1944.

Smith, Al (Allan J.) editor – The Cries of Jesus from the Cross: A Fulton Sheen Anthology. Manchester, New Hampshire: Sophia Institute Press, 2018, ISBN 9781622826209.

Title: The Seven Words to the Cross — The Seven Last Words and the Art of Understanding Difficult People

Fulton J. Sheen; compiled by Allan J. Smith.

Description: Midland, Ontario: Bishop Sheen Today, 2021

Includes bibliographical references.

Identifiers:
ISBN: 978-1-998229-39-0 (paperback)
ISBN: 978-1-737189-04-6 (eBook)

ISBN: 978-1-9902427-77-0 (hardcover)

Subjects: Jesus Christ — The Seven Last Words — Sinners – Selfish – Humanists – Moderns

DEDICATED TO

Mary Queen of the Holy Rosary

IN HUMBLE PETITION
THAT THROUGH THY IMMACULATE
HEART
THE WORLD MAY FIND ITS WAY BACK
TO THE SACRED HEART
OF THY DIVINE SON

*Ad maiorem Dei gloriam
inque hominum salutem*

Jesus calls all His children to the pulpit of the Cross, and every word He says to them is set down for the purpose of an eternal publication and undying consolation.

There was never a preacher like the dying Christ.

There was never a congregation like that which gathered about the pulpit of the Cross.

And there was never a sermon like the Seven Last Words.

Archbishop Fulton J. Sheen

THE SEVEN LAST WORDS OF CHRIST

The First Word
"Father, Forgive Them For They

Know Not What They Do."

The Second Word
"This Day Thou Shalt Be

With Me In Paradise."

The Third Word
"Woman, Behold Thy Son;

Behold Thy Mother."

The Fourth Word
"My God! My God!

Why Hast Thou Forsaken Me?"

The Fifth Word
"I Thirst."

The Sixth Word
"It Is Finished."

The Seventh Word
"Father, Into Thy Hands

I Commend My Spirit."

CONTENTS

PREFACE

*"I have learned more from the
crucifix than from any book."*
St. Thomas Aquinas

ARCHBISHOP FULTON J. SHEEN was a man
for all seasons. Over his lifetime, he spent
himself for souls, transforming lives with the
clear teaching of the truths of Christ and His
Church through his books, his radio addresses,
his lectures, his television series, and his many
newspaper columns.

The topics of this much-sought-after
lecturer ranged from the social concerns of the
day to matters of faith and morals. With an easy
and personable manner, Sheen could strike up
a conversation on just about any subject,
making numerous friends as well as converts.

During the 1930s and '40s, Fulton Sheen
was the featured speaker on The Catholic Hour
radio broadcast, and millions of listeners heard
his radio addresses each week. His topics
ranged from politics and the economy to
philosophy and man's eternal pursuit of
happiness.

Along with his weekly radio program, Sheen wrote dozens of books and pamphlets. One can safely say that through his writings, thousands of people changed their perspectives about God and the Church. Sheen was quoted as saying, "There are not one hundred people in the United States who hate the Catholic Church, but there are millions who hate what they wrongly perceive the Catholic Church to be."

Possessing a burning zeal to dispel the myths about Our Lord and His Church, Sheen gave a series of powerful presentations on Christ's Passion and His seven last words from the Cross. As a Scripture scholar, Archbishop Sheen knew full well the power contained in preaching Christ crucified. With St. Paul, he could say, "For I decided to know nothing among you except Jesus Christ and him crucified" (1 Cor. 2:2).

During his last recorded Good Friday address in 1979, Archbishop Sheen spoke of having given this type of reflection on the subject of Christ's seven last words from the Cross "for the fifty-eighth consecutive time." Whether from the young priest in Peoria, Illinois, the university professor in Washington, D.C., or the bishop in New York, Sheen's messages were sure to make an indelible mark on his listeners.

Given their importance and the impact they had on society, it seemed appropriate to bring back this collection of Sheen's radio addresses that were later compiled into a book titled *The Seven Words to the Cross* (New York: P.J. Kenedy and Sons, 1944).

On October 2, 1979, when visiting St. Patrick's Cathedral in New York City, Pope John Paul II embraced Fulton Sheen and spoke into his ear a blessing and an affirmation. He said: "You have written and spoken well of the Lord Jesus Christ. You are a loyal son of the Church." On the day Archbishop Sheen died (December 9, 1979), he was found in his private chapel before the Eucharist in the shadow of the cross. Archbishop Sheen was a man purified in the fires of love and by the wood of the Cross.

It is hoped that, upon reading these reflections, the reader will concur with the heartfelt affirmation given by St. John Paul II and countless others of Sheen's wisdom and fidelity. May these writings by Archbishop Fulton J. Sheen evoke in us a greater love and understanding for the people who challenge our faith each day.

THE FIRST WORD
- A Word to Humanists -

THERE ARE MILLIONS of souls in this great country of ours who have no religion whatsoever. Their attitudes vary from an earnest yearning for religion to an intense hatred of it. It is quite possible that all of them could be reduced to seven distinct categories.

Our Lord spoke seven times *from* the Cross — and these are called His Seven Last Words. But those who were on Calvary's Hill that afternoon addressed seven words to Him on the Cross, thus revealing the seven different impacts the Cross makes on souls.

The seven words, which Our Lord spoke *from* the Cross were not specific answers to specific challenges, but they do reveal lessons applicable to the challenge.

The first of seven possible attitudes toward the Cross is that of Humanism, for the first group to challenge the Cross was the Humanists. The term Humanist is here understood in the modern philosophical sense and embraces all those who want a religion without a Cross. They believe that man is naturally good, that progress is inevitable through science, and that human reason by its own effort is able to restore peace to the world and to consciences.

They regard all suggestions about faith, grace, and the supernatural order as impractical and unnecessary. They want an education of self-expression, a God without justice, a morality without religion, a Christ without a Cross, a Christianity without sacrifice, a Kingdom of God without redemption.

These Humanists of our day had their prototypes on Calvary on Good Friday. They were those whom Sacred Scripture calls the "passers-by"; a significant term indeed for it suggests those who never remain long enough with religion to know anything about it, those who think themselves wise because they have had a passing acquaintance with Christ.

It is they who speak the First Word to the Cross: "Vah, thou that destroyest the temple of God, and in three days dost rebuild it; save thy own self: if thou be the Son of God, come down from the Cross" *(Matthew 27:40)*.

He is no sooner on the Cross than they ask Him *to* come down. "Come down from your belief in divinity! Come down from your teaching of hell! Come down from your belief that what God hath joined together no man may put asunder! Come down from your belief that Christ will preserve Peter from the gates of hell even to the consummation of the world! Come down from your belief in infallibility! Come down and we will believe!"

And while the mob jeers, there comes from the Cross the answer: "Father, forgive them, for they know not what they do." They said: "*If* thou be the Son of God." Humanists are certain only of humanity, not of divinity.

But He spoke of God: "Father." they said: "Come down." They judged power by deliverance from pain. He said: "Forgive." He judged power by deliverance from sin. They boasted of their knowledge and superior wisdom, and He reminded them that all their wisdom was ignorance: "They know not what they do."

Religion, the Humanists insist, must be love! And who speaks more of brotherhood than humanists? But they want Love without a Cross. And that Our Blessed Lord seems to imply is impossible, for how shall love forgive without first satisfying justice? Shall love mean, "to let the sinner go on sinning" or shall it mean "to make the sinner sinless"?

A religion without a Cross! That is the essence of Humanism. What we want to do here is not to prove the Humanists wrong, but to try to make them understand the meaning of the Cross and how much it symbolizes the love to God. I speak directly to them.

Humanists: You have humanized God, and thus you have dehumanized man. By denying man is supernatural you have not left him even *natural*. For every man wants to be more than he is.

You have tried to make all men brothers, but have you not forgotten that men cannot be brothers unless they have a common Father, and God cannot be a Father unless He has a Son — to whom we all are patterned as brothers?

Swine are content. But you Humanists are not content with humanity, wherein, like monsters of the deep, man preys on man!

You want humanity to be humane. But if there be no model for humaneness, how shall men be modeled?

Look to your doctrines of man: Whence came that which is best in him if it be not from the Best and Holiest?

In Godless hands, man has withered like a rose without roots.

You make indeed a Republic of Kings, but you have no one to crown or anoint them.

The tragedy of your Humanism is believing that dirty things are clean, that cruel are kind, that hence there is no need of a Cross: "Come down and we will believe." To you, all men are good. There are halos even in hell.

And so on Calvary's Hill, you stand and ask in wisdom for a Christ without a Cross, while He answers: "Forgive!"

Do you not know that to have a world without a Cross is in itself a cross? Do you know a mother worthy of the name who would not, out of love, take the pain of her tender babe as her very own, because she loves? Why then should not Supreme Love, in the face of evil, seek to take the penalty which sin deserves, that the evil might be innocent again?

Then why do you say: "Come down and we will believe"? If He came down, in whom would you believe?

Humanists, why are we at war if it be not because sin is in some human blood, and only in the shedding of just blood can there be remission of that sin?

Why not see then that great evils can be conquered only by a God-made-man upon a Cross? Why do you say: "Come down and we will believe"? For if He came down where would love be? "Greater love than this no man hath, that a man lay down his life for his friends" *(John 15:13).*

To avoid a war, when it alone can preserve justice, is not sanctity, you say, but vile surrender! Then to avoid a Cross which alone can redeem from sin, is not human. It is ignorance of man's great needs.

He that made your eye, shall He not see? He that made your ear, shall He not hear? He that made your soldiers, brave enough to die, may not He Himself be a Captain dying to make wrong right?

Then why do you say: "Come down and we will believe"? Do you believe that you, who out of love of neighbor can sacrifice yourself, can do that which God cannot do? Truly! You know not what you do.

Have you Humanists ever seen Love stand up against brute Force and go down because it would not cease to love? If then you bless the Sermon on the Mount, wherein love was preached, why do you curse the Sermon on the Cross, where Love met hate and died? Is not Calvary inseparable from the Mount, for love preached to evil must be crucified.

Love without Power is destroyed by evil. But Love armed with power will die rather than surrender goodness.

God must suffer too as man suffers. Else how can Love be love if it costs not the Lover? Did not your Goethe say: "If I were God this world of sin would break my heart"? Well, that is just what it did to Christ! It broke His Heart!

Why then, if your love for man is sometimes met by sneer and scorn, do you say to a Christ whose God-love was crucified: "Come down and we will believe"? In what can you believe, if Love must love without a Cross?

Not from any talisman of ancient times, but from heaven itself, has come the Cross. For there is "the Lamb, which was slain from the beginning of the world" *(Revelation 13:8)*. From that primal day when the shedding of a brother's blood cried up to the heavens, to this very hour when the race of Abel lies slain by the jealous brethren of the race of Cain, the spilling of unjust blood cries out to heaven, until God heard, and came down as man to shed His blood, that a man might be more than a man — Aye! A very child of God!

The Cross is eternal! It cannot be dug up; it cannot be taken down! It is the core of creation! It is the root of all our lesser Calvaries! Then why do you say: "Come down and we will believe"?

It is God who gives us the Cross. And it is the Cross that gives us God.

You want the Cross but not the crucifix. The cross you wear can be a charm, but the crucifix cannot. Somehow, when you see it, you feel involved! A statue of Buddha does not stir you. Put a crucifix on your desk for three days, and see what it does to you!

Humanists! Remember the days of the French revolution, when a mob swept into the Tuilleries, through room after room it went, destroying. Then, through a closed door, and, lo and behold a chapel! Above the tabernacle hung the crucifix. A hush fell upon the enraged mob. Someone cried: "Hats off." Every head was bowed, then every knee was bent. Indifference was impossible. Then a humanist took the crucifix down, hung it in an adjoining house, and the wild tide of destruction rolled on! They had taken the Christ down from the Cross! Now they could proceed! Religion now was comfortable!

No wonder men want Christ to come down! They want a Cross but not a crucifix. A crucifix perils your soul. You stand unmoved before the Sphinx — but the Christ on His Cross involves you in Its guilt.

Suppose the Christ upon that Cross came down as you bade! He would have forced you then to do His will; and where then would be your freedom? One day He will come without His Cross! Bearing it rather than being borne! But that will be to judge and strike and not to heal, as now; for then the time of healing will be past!

The human never long remains the Humanist, for either beast or angel he becomes, but not just man! If you came from the beast, you cannot leave the beast behind. But if you came from God, then you can leave humanity behind and be a child of God! This is true Humanism, where man finds his center in his Source.

Before 'tis too late, dear Humanists, desist your plea: "Come down and we will believe." But harken: "Father! Forgive." Forgiveness is not cheap. If He offered it without a Cross, you would not take it. But from a nail-pierced hand, how could you refuse? That Cross is the price God paid to buy you from your sins. Without it, there is neither sin nor God.

As you rise in the scale of nobility, do you not choose pain and trouble rather than comfort and ease? Then why not choose Him who did just that for you?

THE SECOND WORD
- A Word to the Sinners -

THERE ARE TWO WAYS of coming to God: through the preservation of innocence; and through the loss of it. Some have come to God because they were good, like Mary, who was "full of grace"; like Joseph, the "just man"; like Nathaniel, "in whom there was no guile"; or like John the Baptist, "the greatest man ever born of woman."

But others have come to God who were bad like the young man of the Gerasenes "possessed of devils," like Magdalen, out of whose corrupt soul the Lord cast seven devils; and like the thief at the right who spoke the second word to the Cross.

The world loves the mediocre. The world hates the very good and the very bad. The good are a reproach to the mediocre, and the evil are a disturbance. That is why Christ was crucified with thieves. Seven hundred years before, Isaiah had prophesied that He would be "reputed with the wicked" *(Isaiah 53:12)*. Luke verified it: "And with the wicked was he reckoned" *(Luke 22: 37)*.

So it was willed by God. This is His true position: Jesus among the worthless ones. During his life He was accused of eating and drinking with sinners; now they can accuse Him of dying with them. And these companions on their crosses were not political prisoners, nor castoff capitalists from a proletarian revolution; they were just plain bandits — pure and simple.

Here is a supreme instance of the Right Man in the right place: Christ among the bandits; the Redeemer in the midst of the unredeemed; the Physician among the lepers — for God does not work through culture but through grace. He does not ask men to be refined; He asks them to be penitent. Thus does God show that we become great not because of what we are, but because of what He gives.

God in His Infinite Wisdom had reached deep into the lower layers of humanity and picked out of its dregs two worthless derelicts, and He used one of them as the escort of His Eternal Son.

At the beginning of the Crucifixion, they both cursed and blasphemed the Saviour. But suddenly the soul of one, lighted by fires from that Central Cross, turned to a King who was being mocked and asked to be one of His subjects: "Lord, remember me when thou shalt come into thy kingdom" *(Luke 23:42).*

Lord: He called Him Lord! A real King is so easy to approach!

Remember me: There was a touch of humor in asking God to remember. God had remembered him before he was born. That is why He is immortal. God had been following his soul down the corridors of time, and now the pursued asks the Pursuer to remember.

When thou shalt come into thy kingdom: How did the thief know He had a Kingdom? Maybe the crown of thorns spoke of a diadem, the crucifixion of a coronation, the nails of a sceptre, and the blood of royal purple. We can never judge people by the way they are dressed!

No prayer to God is ever unanswered. From the Central Cross there flashed back: "This day thou shalt be with me in Paradise" *(Luke 23:43).*

This day: Evil has its hour, but God has His day.

Thou: "And he calleth his own sheep by name *(John 10:3).* This was the foundation of Christian Democracy. The soul of an outcast is of such value that the Eternal Word addresses him in the second person singular: "Thou."

Shalt be with me in Paradise: I wonder why He said in Paradise? To be with Him is Paradise.

The mob on Calvary asked Him to come down from the Cross: the thief asked to be taken up! The masses would have believed if He preached a religion without a Cross; the thief found his faith by hanging on a cross. This is the supreme instance of one bringing good out of evil. It is doubtful if the thief would have found Goodness otherwise!

Why is it that this thief found salvation? Why, on the other hand, did Our Lord say to the chief priests and the ancients: "Amen I say to you, that the publicans and the harlots shall go into the kingdom of God before you" *(Matthew 21:3)*? Why did He lash out with whips at the merchants, and with His tongue scourge the so-called good people, calling them a "brood of vipers" and "whitened sepulchres"? And while speaking harshly to this group, why did he speak so kindly to the woman with five husbands, so gently to the publican Matthew, and so courteously to the good thief?

It can only be because the capacity for conversion is greater in the really wicked than in the self-satisfied and complacent. The very emptiness of soul of the sinners is in itself an occasion for receiving the compassion of God.

Self-disgust is the beginning of conversion, for it marks the death of pride.

The prodigal began to be converted only when he was hungry: "There was a famine." He had left the Father's House saying: "Give me," but he came back saying: "Father, *make me* one of thy hired servants." As the Mother of Our Lord had said of her Son: "He hath filled the hungry with good things; and the rich he hath sent empty away" *(Luke 1:53).*

May it not be that the conversion of the good thief is the key to the conversion of the modern world? Men will return to God, not because they are good, but because they recognize that they are evil. They will come to God through evil rather than through goodness. Or shall we say they will come to God through the Devil.

Countless are the instances mentioned in the Gospel of those who came to God after Satan was driven from their souls. The French Revolutionist Sorel predicted that the basic problem of the twentieth century would be the problem of evil.

The 19th century foreshadowed this in two of its most outstanding writers: Dostoevski, the Russian, and Nietzsche, the German. Nietzsche, representing one side of the problem of evil, believed that the world must pass from

Christ to anti-Christ; Dostoevski, representing the other side, believed that the world would be saved by passing from anti-Christ to Christ.

Most typical of the latter approach is Professor C.E.M. Joad of the University of London, who explains the fanaticism for such creeds of Nazism, Fascism, and Communism as the yearning of irreligious minds to fill up the moral vacuum in their souls by an object of absolute adoration — an evil god.

The universality of evil throughout the world frightened Joad, and "so pervasive and insistent have these evils become that it is at times difficult to avoid concluding that the Devil has been given a longer rope than usual for the tempting and corrupting of men."

None of the explanations given by his contemporaries concerning evil are satisfactory. The socialist explanation of evil in terms of economic inequality and injustice, Joad rejects; for if poverty is the root of all evil, then money must be the source of all virtue.

The psychological explanation of evil attributes evil to suppressed desires, thwarted sex libidos, and mother libidos, all of which could be abolished by popularizing aesthetics, by extending the blessings of the machine and the ballot.

These he rejected after asking himself: "Was no rich man ever cruel, was no unrepressed man ever tyrannical," "was no self-expressive child selfish"?

With the posing of the question, there begins to file before the mind's eye that long line of absolute rulers, the sultans, the caliphs, the emperors and the kings, with the smaller fry, the school masters and the work house superintendents, and the slave overseers, the Squeerses and Brooklehursts, and Bumbles and Murdestones, bringing up the rear of the melancholy procession, who had money enough to be exempt from the cramping effects of poverty and power enough to be free from the repressive effects of authority.

Yet they used their power to increase, and often deliberately to increase, the misery of human beings with such consistency as to provoke Lord Acton's terrible verdict: "All Power corrupts and absolute power corrupts absolutely."

None of the modern explanations of evil, Joad argues, explains the fact of evil. "Evil is not merely a by-product of unfavorable circumstances; it is too wide-spread and too deep-seated to admit of any such explanations; so wide-spread, so deep-seated that one can only conclude that what the religions have taught is true, and that evil is *endemic in the heart of man.*"

"Endemic in the heart of man!" That is it. It is in our blood! It flows through our veins! It gives life to the brain when it thinks evil; it energizes the will when it kills; it fires the muscle when it drops bombs, and it persecutes the prayerful.

In the face of that evil which is endemic in the human heart, this truth emerges: It is one thing to be blind and another thing to know it.

There is hope for those who are deaf and who want to hear and for the lame who want to walk, and there is hope for the diseased who acknowledges the need of a physician and the sinner who feels the need of a redeemer.

The thief at the right conquered evil that way: By admitting his emptiness of soul, he called upon God to save him! There is only one thing in the world worse than sin, and that is denying that we are sinners.

The tragedy of the modern world is that so many deny sin. Never before in the history of the world was there so much evil, and never before was there so little consciousness of it. Talk to a modern man about reconciling his soul with God, and he will say: "What have I ever done to Him? I let Him alone, why should He not leave me alone?"

Why does he say this? For the same reason, a healthy man would say to a surgeon who wanted to operate on him: "There is nothing wrong with me. Leave me alone." In like manner, if you are your own law, if you set your own standards, and if you are your own god, then it is nonsense to ask to be reconciled to another god.

As a man gets more wicked, he understands his wickedness less and less, just as when a man's fever climbs to a point of deliriousness, he understands his sickness less and less. He may even think himself so healthy that he wants to go to work. A moderately bad man always thinks he is good. We never know we were asleep until we wake up, and we never know what sin really is until we get out of it.

Only when you are sick, do you ask for a physician; and only when you recognize yourself as a sinner, do you ask for your Redeemer. Our Lord said: "They that are in health need not a physician, but they that are ill" *(Matthew 9:12)*.

When, therefore, you reach a point where you cease calling yourself "idiotic" (and don't mean it) — and begin to call yourself a "rotter" (and mean it) — you are on the pathway of the good bandit that leads to conversion. The perception of guilt is the condition of conversion, as the perception of disease is the condition of remedy. So long as we think we are good, we will never find God.

If therefore we think that we know it all, how can God teach us what we do not know?

We admit sometimes that we are ill tempered, or that we are intemperate, but will we ever admit that we are proud? We condemn pride so vociferously in others, but we deny that we have ever been guilty. The more conceited we are, the more we hate conceit in others. The more we say, "I am not conceited," the more we prove that we are conceited.

Our pride makes us look down on people so that we can never look up to God. In fact, because our pride admits no law and no authority other than ourselves, it is essentially anti-God.

All our other sins can be from ourselves; for example, avarice, lust, anger, and gluttony. But pride comes direct from hell. By that sin fell the angels. It destroys the very possibility of conversion.

If therefore we can humble ourselves as did the thief at the right, and admit we have done wrong, then out of our creative despair we can cry to the Lord to remember us in our misery! The very moment we stop shutting and posing and begin to see ourselves as we really are, then in our humility, we shall be exalted.

Let us examine our consciences. Let us ask ourselves not how *much* we know, but how much we do not know; not how good we are, but how bad we are. Let us judge ourselves not by the knowledge we possess, but by our consciences; not by our education, but by our habits; not by our politeness, but by our hearts.

As soon as we feel a great void in our souls, and realize that by our sinning we are no longer our own, and acknowledge that we are still thirsty at the border of a well, and admit that we have played the fool and that our follies of the years mount up in their dark arrears, then out of a dark and swampy soul, we cry out with the thief — as all Catholics do when we go to Confession — "Bless me Father, for I have sinned" — "I am a sinner."

Such is the beginning of salvation. The thief died a thief, for he stole Paradise. And if we win Paradise, we will be thieves too, for we will never deserve what we got — the God of everlasting peace!

SEVEN WORDS TO THE CROSS

THE THIRD WORD
- The Selfish -

THE THIRD GROUP IN the world who need to feel the impact of the Cross are the selfish.

By the selfish is here understood all those who feel that salvation is either an individual matter or else the concern of a particular class; that religion has no other right to exist than to remove the impediments of a selfish existence by slum clearance, social security, more playgrounds; and that all else, such as the regeneration of man from sin, or the culture of the soul, is a snare and a delusion.

When the selfish become learned they define religion, in the language of a contemporary philosopher, as "what a man does with his own solitariness"; when the selfish are in distress, they ask "why should God do this to me?" when the selfish sin, they say, "What harm does my sin do to anyone else?"

The selfish were on Calvary's hill in their representative who was the thief on the left! He had heard the blasphemy and pride of his companion thief broken when out of a consciousness of sin he called to the Lord for mercy, but the experience left him untouched. One can be so close to God physically and yet miss Him spiritually.

Turning to the Lord on the Central Cross, the thief on the left, in the supreme expression of selfishness, cried out with bitterness of soul: "If thou be Christ, save thyself and us" *(Luke 23:29)*.

He was the first Marxist! Long before Marx, he was saying "Religion is the opium of the people."

A religion that thinks only of souls when men are dying, which bids them look to God at the moment when the courts are inflicting injustice, which talks about "pie in the sky" when stomachs are empty and bodies racked with pain, which talks about forgiveness when the social outcasts — two thieves and a despised proletarian, a village carpenter — are dying on a scaffold, is a religion that is the opium of the people.

"Save thyself and us" — How modern! Salvation is for a class! Not everyone! Communism speaks only for the proletariat: "Save thyself and us." Fascism speaks only for the nation: "Save thyself and us." Nazism speaks only for the race: "Save thyself and us."

The rich speak only for their class: "Save thyself and us."

Not a word about the salvation of the world, about His people whom He loved, about the Gentiles to whom He would send His Apostles; and above all else, not a word about His beloved Mother beneath His cross whose heart was already pierced by seven swords.

If there was to be salvation for the thief on the left it was not to be spiritual or moral, but physical: "Save thyself and us!" Save what? Our souls? No! Man has no soul! Save our bodies! What good is religion if it cannot stop pain, step down from a gibbet, rescue a class, or pamper selfish interests? Christianity is either a social gospel, or it is a drug.

Our Lord did not answer that selfish thief directly, but He did answer Him indirectly when, looking down from the Cross, He addressed Himself to the two most beloved creatures on earth — Mary, His Mother, and John, His Disciple. But He did not address them as "Mary" and as "John."

If He had called them by their names, they would have remained what they were; representatives of a certain class. If He had said "Mother," she would have been His Mother and no one else's. If he had said "John," he would have been the son of Zebedee, and the son of no one else. So He called Mary "Woman" and John "Son." "Woman, behold thy son . . . son behold thy mother" *(John 19:26-27)*.

He was saying that religion is not what a man does with his solitariness, but what he does with his relationships. And as if to prove for all time that religion is not selfishness, either of an individual or a "set" or a class, He called Mary and John into a relationship as wide as the world. In a certain sense, He de-classified them.

She was no longer to be His Mother alone. As He was the new Adam, she would be the new Eve. He had told her about a year and a half before that there were other ties than those of flesh and blood, namely, the spiritual bond among those who do the will of God. "Behold my mother and my brethren. For whosoever shall do the will of God, he is my brother, and my sister and mother" *(Mark 3:34-35)*.

Now He establishes that new relationship. As she was His Mother by the flesh, she would now be the mother of all "who are born, not of blood, nor of the will of the flesh, nor of the will of man, but of God" *(John 1:13)*.

To herald her in this new relationship as the Mother of Christians, He calls her "Woman" — it was a high summons to universal motherhood.

And John, who up to this point is the son of Zebedee, is not called John — for that would have been to keep the ties of blood. He is addressed as "Son." "son, behold thy mother."

Jesus was the first born of Mary's flesh, but John was the first born of her Spirit at the foot of the Cross; and perhaps Peter was the second, Andrew the third, James the fourth, and we the millionth and millionth born.

He was setting up a new family, a new social relationship. In that context, economic and social questions would be settled, and not otherwise. "Seek ye first the kingdom of God and his justice, and all these things shall be added unto you" *(Luke 12:31).*

Religion is not an individual affair! A man can no more have an individual religion than he can have an individual government or an individual astronomy or mathematics. Religion is social and so social is it that it is not limited to the criminal class, as the thief believed, not to any class, race, nation, or color. All these views are too aristocratic.

Snobbery can exist among proletarians as well as among dukes. The new totalitarian systems have produced "blue bloods" just as obnoxious as some of the blue bloods of monarchy.

This word of Our Lord furthermore reveals that all social duties flow out of these spiritual relationships. He did not say: "John, take care of My Mother," nor did He say: "Mary, look after John as you would me." No! Having established a new relationship between Mary and John, namely that of motherhood and sonship, the duties flowed quite naturally.

Religion is made the sharing of responsibilities. Mary had raised her Child, but now she was to adopt others and love them as sons, poor indeed though they were in comparison.

John had fulfilled his sonship to Zebedee, but now he was to take on new duties as her son and so live that he would never do anything of which his Mother would be ashamed.

Mary continued her duty of bearing the burden of others, for we find her on Pentecost in the midst of the Apostles, mothering the Infant Church as she mothered the Infant Jesus.

John too could never forget that word "son" which he heard from the Cross, as we find him some years after the Ascension writing to the Infant Church: "Behold what manner of charity the Father hath bestowed upon us, that we should be called, and should be the sons of God" *(1John 3:1)*.

There is no Messianic race, no Messianic class, no Messianic color. Our Lord died for all men, and thus set up a new series of relationships with God. And from out of this new set of relationships, slum clearance and social justice and all the rest *follow* — but not otherwise.

Hence Our Blessed Lord said nothing about slavery because He knew that slavery would never be eradicated until men saw themselves related to one another on the basis of equality as children of God.

He did not discourse on the need of child clinics. He first proclaimed the value of a child to a pagan world by becoming a child among children.

He said nothing about the necessity of democracy. But He laid the foundation for it when He told Pilate what we, over 1700 years later, wrote in the Declaration of Independence — that all rights and liberties come from God.

He said nothing about the rights of labor. He first dignified it as a vocation by working as a carpenter.

He said nothing about treating servants decently, but He girded Himself with a towel and washed the feet of His own Apostles. "And whosoever will be first among you, shall be the servant of all" *(Mark 10:44).*

The classic example of the effect of the new relationship was the slave Onesimus, who ran away from his master Philemon. The slave came to Paul who made him a Christian. Paul then asked the slave to return to Philemon bearing a note in which Onesimus is called "my own son whom I have begotten in my bands. . . Do thou receive him as my own . . . Receive him . . . not now as a servant . . . but a most dear brother especially to me; but how much more to thee, both in the flesh and in the Lord" *(Philemon 1:10-16)*. He was no longer a slave because he was a Christian.

What barriers St. Paul would have broken down in his League of Nations: "There is neither Jew nor Greek" (that means, no race or political distinction); "there is neither bond nor free" (no economic distinction); "there is neither male nor female" (no sex distinction); "for you are all one in Christ Jesus" *(Galatians 3:28)*.

When Chile and Argentina were about to go to war, it was the suggestion of a woman that the cannon of the two nations be melted, made into a statue of Christ and placed in the Andes at the border of each and be called "The Christ of the Andes." And it bears this inscription: "Sooner shall these mountains crumble than this pact of peace, entered into at the feet of

Christ between these two nations, shall be broken." And that pact has never been broken!

Some day someone will read the Gospel: "Thou shalt love thy neighbor as thyself"; that is, love the other's interest as you do self-interest. Not until all groups see themselves as bound in a new relationship to the common good, will they sacrifice their own special interests.

So long as every individual exists for himself, we shall have social discontent; so long as every class seeks only its own interest we shall have class warfare; and so long as each nation seeks its own interest exclusively, we shall have war.

After listening to that third word to the Cross, we know that the equal distribution of economic goods does not make men brothers, but that, by making men brothers under the Fatherhood of God, economic goods are distributed. Equality of possessions does not make men brothers, but being brothers makes for economic equality.

The Prodigal Son thought he could have peace through distribution of economic wealth, but it was not until he had restored relations with his father that the distribution worked.

Communism of things will never work until we start with a communism of personal relationships. Individual selfishness cannot be corrected by class selfishness. Selfishness is insanity.

The author of Peer Gynt writes of the inmates of an insane asylum: "It is here that men are most themselves — themselves and nothing but themselves — sailing with outspread wings of self. Each shuts himself in a cask of self, the cask stopped with the bung of self and seasoned in a well of self. None has a tear for the other's woes or cares what any other thinks."

Centering on self, they hate themselves. Doing always what they like, they hate what they do. Having their own way, they block the way and lose their way. Unable to get along with themselves, they cannot get along with anyone else.

No wonder a young product of a progressive school once asked: "Must I always do what I want to do?" It is by no accident that this age which believed in self-expression has ended in self-disillusionment and disgust.

Our Lord spoke to the hating, raging, anti-Christian Saul on the Damascus road: "Saul, Saul, why persecutest thou me? It is hard for thee to kick against the goad" *(Acts 26:14).* He used the figure of an ox hurting itself by kicking against the sharp nails of the cart. He was saying in effect: "When you rebel against Me, you are rebelling against yourself . . . You persecute Me, but you — *you* are perishing."

Men, nations, and systems always destroy themselves by seeking an order other than that based on the brotherhood of all men under the Fatherhood of God! Class consciousness must be transformed into "brother consciousness," or the world will perish. Freedom from God is really the freedom to destroy ourselves.

To the selfish comes the lesson from the Cross! Begin to live for others, and you will begin to live for self. Religion implies social relationships.

We did not wait until we were twenty-one and then, after studying the Constitution, decide to become Americans. We were born American — born out of the womb of America. So likewise, in the spiritual order, we are born out of the womb of the Church. It is the Church founded by Christ which makes us Christian; it is not you or me, as a Christian, who adds our individuality to other individuals to form an institution!

Never, therefore, say: Religion is a purely personal matter. You can no more have your personal religion than you can have your personal sun. If your personal religion unites you to God, and my personal religion unites me to God, then is there not a common relationship between us to a common Father?

When we go to a concert, do we not give attention to the music, that is, do we not allow ourselves to be determined by something *outside* ourselves? Do we think that when people attend concerts, each one should do whatever he pleases, call out his own selections, take the baton from the conductor, or whistle his own tune?

Then why, when the subject is religion, where the Conductor is God, should we insist on our own individual ideas, or say religion is "what I think about God." Rather, religion is what God wants it to be. Hence I must seek His will, not mine, discover His truth, not my opinion.

Nor is it true to say: "The way I conduct my own life is nobody's business but mine," or "it harms nobody else." Could you throw a stone in the sea without causing ripples which would affect even the most distant shore? How then do we think our moral actions can be devoid of social repercussions?

Morality is essentially a relationship of a threefold character: a relationship between my self and my conscience, between my self and my neighbor, and between my self and my God.

You cannot think of a single wrong deed in the world which does not disturb all three relationships — even secret sins. Take, for example, a strong hatred which never expresses itself in violence.

First, it disturbs your relation to yourself; physically, by upsetting your stomach, spiritually by creating a tension between an ideal and a failure to attain it, and morally, later on, by remorse of conscience.

Secondly, it disturbs your relation to your neighbor, by diminishing the content of love in the world. And if enough individuals did exactly what you did, it could cause a war.

Thirdly, it disturbs your relation to God, for if I am a motor made by God which runs best on the fuel of Divine Love which God supplies, it follows that I upset both myself and my happy relation to Him by trying to run the motor on the fuel of hate.

All quarrels, disagreements, wars, strifes, and dissensions begin with a false declaration of independence — independence from God and independence from fellowman.

That incidentally is why the Jews on the one hand, and the Christians on the other, are on the wrong track when they try to break down intolerance by protests within their own group.

The Jews will never crush anti-Semitism so long as they protest against intolerance only within their ranks, or within their press, and completely ignore the intolerance shown to Christians. And the same is true of Christians. Not until they both protest out of a common relationship until the Jew defends the Christian and the Christian the Jew, will there be peace.

One of the reasons why there has been such a great decline of belief in the Divinity of Christ outside the Church is because a proper understanding of the relationship existing between Christ and His Mother has been destroyed.

Would you, as a son, have much regard for anyone who said he liked you, but who refused to speak to your mother? Well, do you think Our Lord can feel any differently, particularly since He gave His Mother to us on the Cross?

Why not then, as a remedy for all selfishness, begin seeing ourselves bound to one another in every increasing relationship, first as common creatures of God, then as sons of the Heavenly Father, as brothers of Christ, as members of His Mystical Body vivified by one Spirit, governed by one Head, and as children of Mary, Our Mother, to whom — as her children who never grow up — we say in the language of Mary Dixon Thayer:

Lovely Lady dressed in Blue
Teach me how to pray!
God was just your little Boy,
Tell me what to say!

Did you lift Him up, sometimes,
Gently, on your knee?
Did you sing to Him the way
Mother does to me?

Did you hold His hand at night?
Did you ever try
Telling stories of the world?
O! And did He cry?

Do you really think He cares
If I tell Him things —
Little things that happen? And
Do the Angel's wings

Make a noise? And can He hear
Me if I speak low?
Does He understand me now?
Tell me for you know!

Lovely Lady dressed in Blue.
Teach me how to pray!
God was just your little Boy,
And you know the way.

A Child on His Knees
© *Macmillan Co., New York*

THE FOURTH WORD
- The Intelligentsia -

EVERY AGE HAS ITS intelligentsia, and by the intelligentsia is here meant not the educated, but those who have been educated beyond their intelligence. A sponge can hold so much water; a person can hold so much education. When the point of saturation is reached in either, the sponge becomes a drip, and the person a bore.

All intelligentsia are proud because of the alleged superiority which their learning gives them. Their judgment of others is based on what they know rather than by conscience.

Religion, they judge by their own standards, and, whenever they write on the subject, their articles are entitled: "My idea of religion." Never do they seek to know God's idea of religion. Their own preconceived prejudices constitute the norm of judgment.

In the 17th century, the intelligentsia believed that any religion was acceptable which satisfied *individual* ideas of interpretation; in the 18th century, the intelligentsia believed that any religion was acceptable on condition it agreed with rational principles of their own making; in the 19th century, they believed any religion was good if it corresponded with their views on politics.

They claim that no educated person can believe in religion, for religion belongs in the same category as folklore, superstition, primitive taboos, and phobias. In the face of real learning, they talk comparative religion; in the face of simple faith, they mock and sneer. Voltaire always believed mockery was the best tool to destroy the infamy of Christianity.

The hall mark of culture is, to the intelligentsia, to be irreligious or anti-religious. They once doubted the existence of God, but nothing else; now they doubt not only themselves but the worthwhileness of humanity.

What impact does the Cross of Christ make upon them? One needs only to go to their intellectual progenitors to study their reaction.

The Fourth Word addressed to the Cross came from the intelligentsia of the time — the Chief Priests, Scribes, and Pharisees: "He saved others; himself he cannot save. If he be the king of Israel, let him now come down from the cross, and we will believe him. He trusted in God; let him now deliver him if he will have him; for he said: I am the Son of God" *(Matthew 27:42-43).*

The intelligentsia always know enough about religion to distort it, hence they took each of the three Titles which Christ had claimed for Himself, "Saviour," "King of Israel," and "Son of God," and turned them into ridicule.

"*Saviour*": So he was called by the Samaritans. Now they would admit He had saved others — probably the daughter of Jairus, and the son of the widow of Naim, and Lazarus. They could afford to admit it now, for the Saviour Himself stood in need of salvation. "Others He saved, Himself He cannot save." The conclusive miracle to them was still lacking.

Poor fools! Of course, He cannot save Himself. The rain cannot save itself if it is to bud the greenery. The sun cannot save itself if it is to light a world; the soldier cannot save himself, if he is to save his country. And Christ cannot save Himself if He is to save His creatures.

"*King of Israel*": That title the crowd gave Him after He fed the multitude, and fled into the mountains alone. They repeated it again on Palm Sunday when they strewed branches beneath His feet. Now that title was mocked as they sneer: "If He is King of Israel, let Him come down from the Cross."

Must all the Kings of earth be seated on golden thrones? Suppose Israel's King decided to rule from a cross, to be King not of their bodies through power, but of their hearts through love? Their own literature was full of the idea of a King Who would come to glory through humiliation.

How foolish then to mock a King because He refuses to come down from His throne. And if He did come down, they would be the first to say, as they did before that, He did it through the power of Beelzebub.

"Son of God," "He trusted in God," "Let God deliver Him if He wants Him, for He said: 'I am the Son of God' ": Irreligious forces have their holiday in moments of great catastrophe. In war time, they ask: "Where is Thy God now?" Why is it that in time of trouble, God is always put on trial and not man? Why in war, should the judge and the culprit change places as man asks: "Why does not God stop the war?"

Our Lord was robbed of the privilege of *acting* freely when they fettered Him with ropes and riveted Him with steel. He was robbed of the privilege of *speaking* freely when the soldier with a mailed fist in the court of Caiphas struck Him a blow on the cheek. He is now robbed of the privilege of *thinking* freely, as the intelligentsia laugh Him to scorn.

There is something of the mockery of hell in their sinister, diabolical language. Mockery is the greeting of hell, for having turned against

God, souls in hell turn against one another, as man becomes a wolf to man.

A man literally consumes every other man; one lost soul preys fiendishly on the soul of his neighbor. The one who is nearest is always the one who is farthest away. It is the law of hell, that one hates his neighbor.

As criminals when caught in the net of justice turn against one another, so those who stumble into the realm of eternal darkness, gloat over the misery of every other soul in the region of death.

Thus did Christ hear Himself mocked! They do not know that they are already lost. They think He is. Therefore they, the really damned, mock one whom they believe is damned. Hell was triumphing in the human! Truly this was the hour of the power of the devils of hell.

To all the good on earth who have been mocked because of their faith in God — you are not without an example. The sneer you receive in the office because out of love for this Good Friday Passion of your Saviour, you abstain from meat on Friday; the turned up lips and the barbed laughter you suffer because you pray, or because of your loyalty to the Church; the ridicule of your fellow soldiers as you kneel at your cot in the barracks and pray — all these are but echoes of the taunts your Lord received on Calvary.

But do not come down from your cross! "Be glad and rejoice, for your reward is very great in heaven" *(Matthew 5:12)*. "If we suffer we shall also reign with Him. If we deny Him, He will also deny us" *(2Timothy 2:12)*.

Why does not He Who is the morning star, put out the darkness of this hour? Because this is a moment when He wills to make atonement for the sins of men. The essence of sin is twofold: it involves a turning *from* God, and a turning *to* creatures.

He Who is without sin now wills to feel the two effects of sin. Because sin involves turning to creatures, He suffers *at the hand of men*: because sin involves a turning from God, He permits Himself to feel that Divine abandonment, as in the midst of rasping mockery He cries with a loud voice: "My God! My God! Why hast Thou Abandoned Me?"

This is His answer to the intelligentsia. Let them take their thought off learning for the moment and concentrate on conscience and its sin. Sin is separation from God! Sin is supreme loneliness! Sin separates man from God, man from man.

This disruptive power of sin which is permanent in hell, He now allows to devastate

His inmost soul that He might suffer what we deserve for our sins.

That is why He left the mockery of hell unanswered, and the scorn of the intelligentsia unchallenged. The Scriptures say: "God will not be mocked." God will be mocked in the beginning! Not in the end!

That fellowship between God and man which was broken by sin, He now wills to feel as His own as His cry reveals that the essence of sin is not a mission, but a dismissal. This is what sin deserves: mockery from men, rejection by God. Such is the worm and fire of hell.

Think not that the cry of abandonment meant that He Who takes upon Himself the sins of the world, is not the Son of God. God could not be abandoned by God.

But God in the form of man could be abandoned, for in the strong language of St. Paul: "Christ hath redeemed us from the curse of the law, being made a curse for us: for it is written: Cursed is everyone that hangeth on a tree" *(Galatians 3:13)*. The very words he quoted were taken from a Psalm written thousands of years before prophesying the very mockeries now hurled against the Cross!

The Son of David was quoting the songs of David. He Who is the Son of God was stirring the waters of the Son of Man with His own

Spirit. The word made flesh was having recourse to His own words. The poet was reciting His own poetry.

It was the poetry of Redemption. The courts of justice, the mobs, the unrepentant, the intelligentsia had now done all they could to break Him down, by throwing back all His Love in His Face, but that Great Royal Love remains unbroken. For in the very dark moment when He felt the isolation and abandonment which sin merited, He in His human nature calls on God.

The way back to God for the intelligentsia is here indicated from Man's side and from God's.

(A) On man's side, that cry "My God" is the antithesis of the pride of the intelligentsia. It is a cry of humility and primordial obedience. Having arrived at the lowest depths of loneliness, man still asks for the right of being human. It is the confession of a duty-bound child; a prayer so subservient that man continues to seek God even in the darkness of abandonment.

Here Christ, taking on man's sin, asks God to deal justly with a creature predestined to be a child, and to open the door to the prodigal again. Sinful man is knocking! Adam hid after his sin. God asked: "Where art thou?" Now, the new Adam lays hold of Adam's loneliness of soul and asks God: "Where art Thou?"

This is the foundation of religion and the way of salvation to all the intelligentsia, viz.: by becoming obedient; by making a total surrender to God; by acknowledging creaturehood; by pleading for restored fellowship.

A man can thus feel the pains of hell, mockery, and loneliness and still ask God why he is not acceptable in heaven. Nor in His word is there unbelief in misery or in the midst of the penalties of sin; never "is there a God" or even "God," but "My God, My God."

By laying oneself bare as the needy child, who cannot live in the loneliness of sin, man can still prove he takes no delight except in God: "For what have I in heaven? and besides Thee what do I desire upon earth?" *(Psalm 72:25).* That cry was the hope of man. It was the denial of the chaotic amidst chaos! We too can take our "Whys" to God!

Then follows the beautifully haunting realization that it really was not God who abandoned us; it was we who abandoned God. Adam hid from God after his sin — so does man. God never really abandons man! Christ in His human nature was never separated from His Divine nature.

Because man is made for God, he feels sin as abandonment. It would be like a man who refused to eat saying: "O Food, why hast thou abandoned me?" Or parched lips of a man walking from a spring saying to the spring: "Water, why hast thou abandoned me?" As the stomach needs food, as parched lips need water, and the mind needs truth, so man needs God. We refuse to drink and then wonder why we are thirsty; we refuse to love God and wonder why we are unhappy.

(B) If the way back to God on man's side is by the acknowledgment of creaturehood, from God's side, the reconciliation is effected through love. Creatures run out of love when over-betrayed and mocked! They touch bottom and say: "I wash my hands of him."

But here Divine Love refuses to leave the sinner even in sin. We have no expression for the opposite of "washing our hands of a person" except "the Lord hath laid on Him the iniquity of us all" *(Isaiah 53:6)*.

To bear sin meant to go on loving even in the midst of a crucifixion.

I can go on sinning despite His love, for I am free. But at the same time, when I see Christ still loving me even when I crucify Him; when I see Him still praying to God for me, even when I abandon Him, and never losing faith in me though I lose faith in Him, *by that very fact* I am made penitent, for how can I go on sinning in the face of love like that?

I may not be at the end of my journey, but I am at the end of my rebellion. I now see the nature of sin and cry: "Why am I abandoned?" I see the nature of God and cry: "My God, My God."

A child sins seriously. A mother suffers because of that sin, and the suffering varies in direct relationship to her love and the gravity of the sin. Because the mother loves the child, she cannot let the child suffer the effects of the sin alone. She enters into it and shares it. If the child sees the mother suffering, it will be drawn to penitence. Then the mother can forgive.

Christ so loved us that He took our sins upon Himself as if He were guilty, and draws us freely to repentance by the price He paid to save us. Hence forgiveness is no glib thing! The Cross was the supreme expression of the righteousness of God!

If the redemption of man were done without cost, it would insult us, for no man with a sense of justice wants to be "let off." It would insult God, for the whole moral order founded on justice would be impugned. The Cross is the eternal proof that no sin is forgiven through indifference.

God safeguards His justice even the very moment He forgives: "All we, like sheep, have gone astray, every one hath turned aside into his own way: and the Lord hath laid on him the iniquity of us all"*(Isaiah 53:6)*. "Him, who knew no sin, he hath made sin for us, that we might be made the justice of God in him" *(2Corinthians 5:21)*.

From the side of man and God, therefore, we come into relationship with God primarily as disobedient sons returning to a Holy and loving Father.

Intelligentsia! You are the most difficult class in the world to bring to God, not because you are wise, for no one is wise unless he has discovered truth.

To the self-wise who rejected Truth, Our Lord said: "the publicans and the harlots shall go into the kingdom of heaven before you" *(Matthew 21:31)*.

Could it be possible that Paul was right in telling the intelligentsia of Corinth that the wisdom of the world is foolishness with God? Is character in the intellect alone, as you believe, or in the will which clings to God even in darkness as this world reveals?

Are all the intelligentsia happy? Are all the uneducated unhappy? Are you right in thinking that so long as a man is intellectually honest, his private morality is of no concern?

May it not be that the modern hatred of religion is to a great extent determined by the way men live? Do not men, in the end, delude themselves by making a creed fit the way they live, rather than making the way they live fit a creed? Is not mockery of religion but a vain attempt to ignore?

Why is it the intelligentsia are more interested in destroying faith in others than in giving others their own incertitude? You have told others that to believe in God is foolishness, but what wisdom did you give as a substitute? Why do you never think of making others better, but only "wiser" according to your own judgment?

A few years ago I instructed a young man in one of the large colleges of the East, which college incidentally was founded to teach religion. His classmates ridiculed him by buying rosaries and swinging them before his eyes as they passed him on the Campus. Why must the intelligentsia mock? Does learning really bring understanding?

Take an hour off tonight and meditate on the answer of Our Lord to the intelligentsia of His time. For all their mocking there was an answer — the total, complete surrender to God

— the smiting of pride into nothingness. "And every height that exalteth itself against the knowledge of God, and bringing into captivity every understanding unto the obedience of Christ" *(2Corinthians 10:5)*. As you examine your conscience, ask yourselves:

Are you your own creator? Do you owe what is deepest in you to no other? Have you any more right than a rose to say there is no life beyond you? Is the freedom of your soul self-originating? Have you never done anything wrong in your life, and do you feel no need of atoning for it?

Did not Our Lord say: "Amen I say to you, unless you be converted and become as little children, you shall not enter into the kingdom of heaven" *(Matthew 18:3)*. By this He meant that you must put on a new mind: He does not ask you to be childish; He asks us to be childlike, i.e., to be docile, to be teachable.

When, therefore, in the darkness, your soul feels disquieted, and your conscience haunts you, think not that this is due to psychological explosions from an unconscious mind; it is rather the call of God.

As you lie awake at night and ponder over your sins, for the darkness brings out your own darkness; as you mourn the loss of relatives or friends and for the moment ponder on the problem of death; as you feel stirred by the purity, sacrifice, and faith of others, even when you ridicule; as you try to throw off a thousand qualms of conscience a day — ask yourself what these promptings really are!

They are actual graces: Divine solicitations, beckoning calls of the Shepherd to lost sheep.

Frustrate them not by introducing speculative questions, as did the woman at the well, when the root of your discontent is in your morals, not in your mind.

If you have been away from the Sacraments twenty years or more, cease justifying your rebellion against God by saying you no longer believe in the Sacrament of Penance. Your quasi-intellectual opposition is a camouflage for your moral cowardice. You are afraid to face your sins; so you attack the creed.

Get down on your knees! Humble yourselves before your God, for He heareth you before you call on Him. He knows your loneliness; He felt it on the Cross. He knows your needs; He bought them on Calvary.

Think not that Love has passed you by; it is only the bowl of human affection you drank dry — not the chalice of salvation.

The Eternal still pleads He refuses to destroy your freedom: "Come to Me all ye who labor and are heavily burdened." A humbled and contrite heart the Master will not despise, and from it may you pray in the language of the ancient prayer:

"Lord, make me an instrument of Thy peace; where there is hatred, let me sow love; where there is injury, pardon; where there is doubt, faith; where there is despair, hope; where there is darkness, light: and where there is sadness, joy."

"O Divine Master, grant that I may not so much seek to be consoled as to console; to be understood, as to understand; to be loved, as to love; for it is in giving that we receive, it is in pardoning that we are pardoned, and it is in dying that we are born to eternal life."

THE FIFTH WORD
-The Moderns -

THE FIFTH GROUP WITH a distinct reaction to religion are the Moderns. The Moderns are those who believe in moderation. They hate excesses either good or evil; compromise is the very essence of life; they have an "open mind" — in fact so open that they never close it on anything absolutely right and true; they are what the Scriptures call "luke-warm," but they prefer to call themselves "broad."

The Moderns are good persons by the standards of the world; they have their daughter married in a Church, where she was never baptized; they like Easter Sunday services and particularly the Fashion Parade which follows; in discussions, they feel that a pretty good case can be made out for the existence of some Power behind the Universe.

They read seven books a year — all novels, chosen because they were either widely advertised or because their neighbor read them; they serve on hospital boards, parent-teachers associations, contribute to birth-control clinics and Russian relief; but always within the limit allowed by income tax.

They send their children to the best schools they can afford; never send them to church, but let them go to the movies at least twice a week; they take their politics from a radio commentator; their economics from their son who has had one year of it under a Marxist Professor in college. They think there are too many divorces, but after all, we are not living in the Middle Ages; they believe that the majority is always right; that religion does add some sentiment and symbolism to life — in a word, they are what their neighbors would call "good" people.

Their words are correct; their manners courteous; they shrink from giving pain to others; they discountenance profligacy; cursing and swearing are vulgar: they are the Good Moderns.

Being sceptical and doubting the very existence of truth they regard any enthusiasm for religion as a folly. Religion for them is more often an occasion for derision than conversion; they boast of their objectivity, but it consists merely in surveying all planets but inhabiting none.

They love to seek truth, but scrupulously avoid the responsibility of finding it; they want to be auditors at all classes, but to be pupils of none; they find it easier to doubt than to examine.

They never want to know whether a thing is right or wrong, but whether it is "progressive" or "reactionary," "liberal" or "contemporary"; they love to make distinctions between the "historical Jesus" and the "Christ of Paul" and say they would be Christian tomorrow if "all the accretions and perversions" were eliminated. They follow that one avocation in life in which there is no apprenticeship — criticism.

Transactions of business speculations in stocks, the ephemeral happenings of the day, the superficial wisdom of commentators — all these find a way directly to their hearts. But religion to them is weariness when it is not humorous. Religion they say makes them melancholy and they want to relax.

What is the reaction of the "moderns" to the Cross? We need only go back to their ancestors who addressed the Fifth Word to the Cross.

The Gospels call them "by-standers at the Cross." These original Moderns loved their puns and their humor at the expense of religion. The occasion for it was the Fourth Word of Our Lord from the Cross: "My God, My God, why hast Thou forsaken Me?" It was spoken in Hebrew: "Eli, Eli, Lemma Savacthani."

The bystanders knew very well what that meant. But to those who willed to mock, it was a fine opportunity for a pun. Pretending that they understood him to say "Eloi" rather than "Eli" or the "Elias" rather than "God," they said: "This man calleth Elias" — "Let us see whether Elias will come to deliver him" *(Matthew 27:47-49) (Mark 15:34-36).* The lance thrust of this word consists in the fact that they make the self-vaunted Messias summon a man who must come before the Messias.

It was a typical attitude of many who think *religion means something else than it actually does*: mistaking Eloi for Eli, Elias for God, religion for social service; contemplation for dreaming; mortification for morbidity; confession for psychoanalysis, and the Papacy for politics. The dilettantes and moderns always think we are calling on Elias when we are actually calling on God.

Their very words indicated passivity, indifference, and false caution: "Let us see if Elias will come to deliver him" *(Matthew 27:49).* Wait! Take your time! Do not do anything rash! Wait and see what the Church does about Marxism! Wait and see if it will change its marriage laws! Do not be in a hurry to give your soul to God!

The difficulties of the moderns are always verbal, never real. Those who remain away from God suffer from confusion of their own making. They think the Church is something else than it is, as the bystanders mistook God for Elias.

It is not what they know that is true, which keeps them from salvation; it is what they know that is wrong! They realize this when they come into the Church. Church windows from the outside look like meaningless lead tracings, but from the inside looking out, they reveal patterns of exquisite beauty and loveliness.

As Our Lord did not answer those who mocked Him in the Fourth Word, neither does He answer those who mock Him now. The perfect soul never permits itself to be drawn down to the level of those who mock, for "mockery is the fume of little hearts."

But He did answer them indirectly. To the bystanders, the dilettantes, the over-cautious moderns, He did give the key to salvation: the need of fire for a cause as burning as thirst.

There is no pain of the human body comparable to thirst. Who has not heard of "the panting thirst that scorches in the breath of those that die the soldier's fiery death"?

For almost Three Hours now He had remained bareheaded, except for a crown of thorns, under that burning blinding sun, while from four fountains there poured out life in the form of blood. It was therefore natural for Him to ask for a drink!

He, the God-man! He, Who shut up the sea with doors as it did burst forth as issuing out of a womb; He, Who threw stars in their orbits and spheres into space; He, Who said: "He that believeth in me shall never thirst" (*John 6:35*); He, Who once stood up in the Temple on the last day of a solemn feast, and cried out in a loud voice: "If any man thirst, let him come to me, and drink" (*John 7:37*), now speaks not to God, nor to the executioners, nor to His Mother, but to man. He asks man for a drink: "I thirst!"

There was genuine thirst there, for no one could be crucified without it. But under that physical symbol of thirst was hidden a spiritual thirst, and St. John who was at the foot of the cross made it known: He spoke that the Scriptures might be fulfilled! What Scriptures? His own words: "I was thirsty, and you gave me to drink" (*Matthew 25:35*). It was, therefore, a thirst to be thirsted for — a thirst for the salvation of souls.

While the bystanders were like ice, He was on fire; while they coursed in shallow streams, He launched out into the deep; while they only stand and wait, He plunges in that one cry through both fire and water; while the Moderns were saying: "Let us see" Our Lord was answering: "No, be athirst! Be afire! I am come to cast fire on the earth: and what will I, but that it be kindled?" *(Luke 12:49)*.

Religion is not for calculating love. One must love life like wine and drink death like water. Religion is love and:

Love is not love
Which alters, when it alteration finds,
Or bends with the remover to remove.
O! No! it is an ever-fixed mark
That looks on tempests, and is never shaken; . . .
Love's not Time's fool, though rosy lips and cheeks
Within his bending sickle's compass come
Love alters not with his brief hours and weeks
But bears it out even to the edge of doom.

William Shakespeare

Our Lord chose persons of that kind for His Disciples: Sons of thunder like James and John, who would have called down lightning from heaven on the Samaritans, but whose zeal once rightly directed, truly thundered through the world.

He chose hot-blooded, fiery, impetuous Peter, swinging a sword recklessly at night, and yet out of love for God, breathing his last on a Cross upside down, thinking it unbecoming to die like the Lord.

He chose Magdalen, passionate and sensuous, the kind of woman who gave her body without giving her soul, and yet the one who under the touch of Christ's fiery hand gave her body in penance to save souls in grace.

There is no place for spineless characters in religion. "I know thy works, that thou art neither cold nor hot. I would thou wert cold, or hot. But because thou art lukewarm and neither cold nor hot, I will begin to vomit thee out of my mouth" *(Revelation 3:15-16)*. Such is God's disdain for the indifferent.

There is more possibility for conversion in a passion wrongly directed, than in indifference. Where there is fire, its direction can be changed by God's grace, so that it will burn upward rather than downward, and thus enkindle goodness rather than vice.

But where there is indifference and false tolerance and spineless broadmindedness that looks at all causes and espouses none — there is no chance.

There are many potential saints in prison and many potential devils in the service of God. In both cases, there is thirst: thirst for Satan or thirst for God. And either thirst could be reversed.

Lenin, for example, was a St. Francis in reverse, as St. Francis was a Lenin in reverse. Both started with the idea of violence: Lenin believed in social reform by violence to a class; St. Francis believed in social reform by violence to himself.

They were both right in their starting point: violence: "The kingdom of heaven suffereth violence, and the violent bear it away" *(Matthew 11:12)*. It was the direction of that violence that made the difference between the two!

Hate and love spring from the same passion, as laughter and sorrow drink from the same fountain of tears. The difference is in the motive and the end for which they live. Religion is something that must be either hated or loved. It cannot be watched!

Too many people get credit for being good when they are only passive. They are too often praised for being broadminded when they are so broadminded they can never make up their minds about anything. They are like the icebergs in the cold streams of the North; they cannot help being icebergs! But let those icebergs get down into the warm gulfstream of the south and yet remain icebergs: then *they* will have character!

Moderns! Wait not for a proof of your own making as did the bystanders at the Cross. They dictated the terms upon which they would accept the Divinity of Christ: you dictate terms upon which you will accept the Divinity of the Church. You are looking for bargains in religion, and there are none.

The Church has never yet had a sale on beliefs; it has never compromised on a single Divine Truth to win a soul. There are plenty of religious shops that have, and that is why today so many of them are ending in bankruptcy.

What is particularly interesting is that those religious shops who compromised on God's Truth to win you Moderns, are the very ones whom you Moderns today reject.

Moderns! The proofs for the Divinity of Christ are never so overwhelming as to destroy your freedom; they are sufficient to convince you, but not to compel you. Christ will never batter down the door of your reason: "Behold, I stand at the door and knock." The latch is on our side of the door, not on God's side.

The proper aim of speculation is not merely to destroy falsehood – but to preserve and consolidate the structure of truth. There is a grave danger in too much analysis:

"Little by little we subtract
Faith and fallacy from fact,
The illusory from the true,
And starve upon the residue."

You may have greater *knowledge* of uncorrelated facts than most people — Moderns often do, but you have done nothing with your *wills*. Did you ever stop to think that there is such a thing as knowledge increasing through love?

You must, of course, first know to love, but then you must love to know, for the knowledge from the outside that comes from investigation is nothing compared to the knowledge that comes from the *inside* by love.

When you know a thing you draw it to yourself; when you love a thing you draw yourself to it.

Have you ever tried to love God even on the basis of the little knowledge that you did have? If you had, your knowledge would have grown by leaps and bounds. "If any man will do the will of him; he shall know of the doctrine, whether it be of God, or whether I speak of myself" *(John 7:17).* You Moderns will never be convinced of religion by argument, for the chances are you have sufficient knowledge. You need *good* will. The best cure for "sceptic poisoning" is love. Develop fire and enthusiasm — God has no use for tepid souls.

Love your neighbor with an unselfish, dedicated, passionate love, and you will find God. Visit the sick in the hospitals, the poor in the slums. Give them some of your possessions, but also listen to them.

Notice the different attitudes of those who have faith and those who lack it; how peaceful some are in suffering, and how rebellious others are. Slowly you will come to see that if God can make so much difference in their lives, what a difference He would make in your own.

Suffer deeply in sympathy with others; love them in an unselfish way, and you will learn more than you ever learned from books. Elias will never come to you, but Christ will come in suffering and in need.

"For I was hungry, and you gave me to eat; I was thirsty and you gave me to drink; I was a stranger and you took me in: naked, and you covered me: sick, and you visited me; I was in prison and you came to me" *(Matthew 25: 35-36)*.

Our Lord said: "I thirst." This was the crucified way of saying "Come to me, all you that labour, and are burdened, and I will refresh you" *(Matthew 11:28)*. God always puts Himself on the attitude of wanting something as an excuse to give us something.

"Give me to drink," He said to the Woman at the well. But He Who asked also said: "If thou didst know the gift of God, and who he is that saith to thee, Give me to drink, thou perhaps wouldst have asked of him, and he would have given thee living water" *(John 4:10)*. He thirsts for us, only because we need Him so! It is not His loss if we love Him not; it is ours.

Without Him our hearts are panting, our lips are parched. Tomorrow we think the rocks of the world will give us fountains, but the next day we find them dry. Each new day brings on its new deception and vain glimmer of the same mirage.

Finally, the Word of Our Lord from the Cross reveals the secret of your unhappiness: it is your moderation. You have no great loves:

you are not on fire; you never thirst. Even we who know the Saviour and His Cross have been infected by your passivity. We have become like you — lukewarm.

The cohorts of Satan today have more passion for the spreading of evil, than many of the children of God have for the spreading of Truth. As Prometheus stole the fire from heaven, so the Pentecostal fires have been stolen from our altars and are now blazing in the temples of anti-God.

All of us are Moderns in a certain sense; we do not love Love as we ought. God is a consuming fire, and we are puny embers. Christ came to cast fire upon the earth, and we throw up a smoke screen.

We are all waiting for Elias to take Him down! Why do we not do it and do it *now*! We go up to Calvary, but we come down uncrucified! Woe! Woe unto us that come down from Golgotha's Hills with hands unscarred and white.

From the Cross, the Saviour cries, I thirst, and we reach Him vinegar and gall. If the Cross means anything, it means that our human goodness is not enough. Well may He say to us:

You call Me Master, and obey Me not.

You call Me Light, and see Me not.
You call Me Way, and walk not.
You call Me Life, and desire Me not,
You call Me Wise, and follow Me not,
You call Me fair, and love Me not,
You call Me rich, and ask Me not,
You call Me eternal, and seek Me not,
You call Me gracious, and trust Me not,
You call Me noble, and serve Me not.
You call Me mighty, and honor Me not,
You call Me just, and feed Me not.
If I condemn thee, blame Me not.

Engraved on an old slab in the
Cathedral of Lubeck, Germany

THE SIXTH WORD
- The Sensationalists -

THE SIXTH IRRELIGIOUS group are the Sensationalists: those for whom religion must always be dramatic, *i.e.*, they judge it by their feelings rather than by their minds and wills; their religion is a titillation rather than a sanctification; a "feeling good" rather than being good; a startling overtone rather than a quiet, subdued minor.

They accuse the Church of doing nothing because it is not doing anything sensational; as they might say, "There is nothing in the papers" because there was no riot, no murder mystery, no scandal in high life and no train wreck.

If, for example, I announced that next Sunday I would broadcast standing on my head to symbolize that the world was topsy-turvy, and if in that ecstasy of modernity, I called the posture "iambic-dithyrambic," I would have most of the newspaper photographers of New York in the studio. Headlines would appear: "Remarkable new symbolism: Father Sheen stands on his head." My radio audience would pick up about 1000 per cent. But if I announced that next Good Friday night I would preach on the Cross, few would listen.

There is nothing so calculated to win many modern minds to religion as playing the fool, catering to the gallery, and making salvation dramatic.

The Sensationalists were represented at the Cross by the Roman soldiers of whom Luke writes: "And the soldiers also mocked him, coming to him, and offering him vinegar and saying: If thou be the King of the Jews save thyself" *(Luke 23:36-37)*.

These men were not Jews, nor citizens of conquered Israel; they were proud legionnaires of Rome's screaming eagles. Why then did they refer to Him mockingly as the King of the Jews? Because in keeping with the spirit of paganism, they thought all gods were national gods.

Babylon had its god; the Medes and Persians had theirs; the Greeks had theirs, and so did the Romans have their own. The implication was that of all the national gods; none seemed poorer and weaker than the God of Israel, Who could not save Himself from a tree.

Their mockery is something like we hear today. "Germany prays to God; America prays to God; England prays to God; On Whose side is God?" The implication being that God must necessarily be a geographical Deity restricted to one people, one race, and one nation.

The answer of course to that taunt is, that if we prayed as we should, we would all be on the same side because the perfect prayer is: "Thy Will be done." The very fact that we ask a question of that kind proves we do not understand that God is the Father of all. Too many are worried about whether God is on our side, and heedless as to whether we are on God's side.

But there was something more significant still in their mockery; these men were sensationalists: hence they expected religion to be dramatic — just as dramatic as unloosening fetters and turning a cross into a throne.

In their eyes, God could justify himself only by doing a stunt, by being eccentric, pandering to their love of excitement. They wanted a Life of Christ like Hollywood might do it, with love scenes between Judas and Magdalen.

That is why they asked Him to step down from the Cross. They wanted an incident that would make them say "Ah" when their eyes saw it, rather than that one which would make them say "I believe" when their minds, under the grace of God, knew it.

All through the ages, there have been groups who despise the unobtrusive in religion. In the Old Testament, Naaman came to Elias the prophet to be cured of leprosy. He expected a dramatic cure. But the man of God told him to "Go and wash in the Jordan." In disgust at such a simple, common-place suggestion, Naaman turned and went away in a rage.

Satan too believes in the dramatic. One of the temptations on the Mount was to suggest to Christ that He throw Himself down from the pinnacle unhurt, summoning to Himself legions of angels bearing Him up lest He dash His Foot against a stone.

And now the sensationalists at the Cross with their jaded appetites, and their sadistic impulses make the same appeal. Come down from the Cross with rosebuds in place of scars, garlands in place of a crown of thorns, and with power instead of sacrifice.

Just suppose He did come down unscarred from that cross. Would these sensationalists have believed? They probably would have summoned a professor from Athens to prove it was all an illusion.

While these soldiers were asking for something as dramatic as the King of the Jews unloosening His manacles of steel, Our Blessed Lord said in His language a very simple word, a word which meant: "The drama is already over." And the word He spoke was a word of quiet triumph: "It is finished."

To those soldiers, it must have been as preposterous as if you came into a theater about 8:30 one evening and while you asked: "When is the curtain going up" — someone on the stage announced: "I am very sorry, the play is over. The curtain is already rung down. You have missed the plot. It is finished."

Sensationalists miss Divinity for just that reason: the true religion is always unspectacular. The foolish virgins go to buy oil for their lamps, and when they come back, they find the Bridegroom already returned. And the door closed. It was so undramatic.

A beautiful maiden knocks at the door of an inn, and an innkeeper tells her there is no room. Into a stable, she enters and there a child is born. It was God's entrance into the world. But it was so undramatic.

A collector of taxes is seated at his table counting money, and a passer-by calls to him: "Come, follow Me." Matthew becomes an Apostle. It was so undramatic.

Three common criminals in the eyes of Roman law carry their crosses up a hill. One of them Our Saviour forgives and rescues him into Paradise. It was so undramatic.

In fact, it was boring. So the soldiers took dice and sat down and shook them to see who would have His garments. There within a stone's throw of them — was being enacted the tremendous drama of redemption, and they only sat and gambled.

All life is a gamble as we only know it! Some throw dice and play for such small stakes, like garments and wealth; others throw a life and play for the stake of eternal salvation.

But it was so undramatic! They missed their play and lost! But the man on the Cross was saying His cause had won. "It is finished."

What did He mean: "It is finished"? Three times this phrase is used in Sacred Scripture: at the beginning of human history, at the end and in the middle of history. At the beginning, for in Genesis, we read: "So the heavens and the earth were *finished*, and all the furniture of them" *(Genesis 2:1)*.

At the end of time, we hear that Word sounding throughout the world: " . . . And there came a great voice out of the temple from the throne saying: It is done" *(Revelation 16:17)*. Between these two extremes, we hear Our Lord on the Cross dividing all history into a period before and after His coming, binding both unto

Himself in this sixth utterance from the Cross: "It is finished."

The Word in humiliation, by Whom the world was made, now takes the world once again into His Hands and surrenders it to the Father saying: The curtain may now go up on the reign of the Spirit. The world is ready for the last act.

This Word so undramatically spoken revealed that Christ was not only true God but also true man.

First, it revealed Him as the Son of God, for as the Eternal Word He was, as it were, making His report to the Father, that the redemption of man was now finished and the time was ripe for the sending of the Holy Spirit into the souls of men to make them children of God. What was so wonderfully created, could now be more marvelously regenerated.

In the beginning of the world God saw that it was good and rejoiced; now the Son sees that it is better and breaks out into a poem of joy: "It is perfected." For "where sin abounded, grace did more abound" *(Romans 5:20)*. "For as by the disobedience of one man, many were made sinners; so also by the obedience of one, many shall be made just" *(Romans 5:19)*. Through all eternity the Father says to His Son: "Thou art my Son, this day have I begotten

Thee." Now the Son says to the Father: "Thou art my Father; this day have I finished it."

This cry of victory also revealed His human nature, for by it the sinner is now acquitted of his sin, the last farthing is paid, the handwriting of debt blotted out and man restored to union with God. All the debts outstanding against man were paid, for being man, He suffered as man.

But being God, His suffering had infinite value. "For God indeed was in Christ, reconciling the world to himself, not imputing to them their sins; and he hath placed in us the word of reconciliation" *(2Corinthians 5:19)*. From now on He can await the Father's rending of the grave on Easter morn, in the final proclamation that it was not He that died; it was sin.

This word was not the sigh of a sufferer finding relief; it was the word of a Divine Artist finishing the work His Father had given Him to do — finished at about the age of 33.

Thus, the perfecting of creation by redemption and the restoration to fallen man of the dignity of Divine adoption was rendered all the more undramatic because He did not finish His Work with an autobiography. Rather, His autobiography was a biography. He did not say: "I finished it"; but "It is finished."

He is not the subject of the Greatest work which was wrought on this poor and sinful earth of ours. The servant Jahoe does not name Himself but rather speaks of the whole Program which God wrought through Him. Nor is He saying: "Thank God I have not been unsuccessful" or "I will be remembered." The "it" rather than the "I" closes an autobiography of the Son, as if it were a biography written by the Father and the Holy Spirit. He could not endure the thought of a book entitled: "My Three Years in Israel."

He is not one of the world's "great men." "Great men" are always dramatic. As if their works needed justification, they ring down the curtain of life with a great "I am." Great men always reveal themselves: This Man on the Cross concealed Himself. Therefore, He was God as well as man.

Sensationalists! Salvation is not sensational. Faith is not emotional; the redemption is not dramatic. You can sit in the very shadow of the Cross as did the soldiers, and still miss its meaning.

You can justify your refusal to come to God because of scandals. So did the soldiers. It was an awful scandal that Christ the Son of God should swing impotent from a peg.

From that quiet, undramatic word that His work was perfected, learn that no one is as unsensational as God. He comes in the zephyrs, not in thunder. Therefore, look for God in the commonplace. That they should seek God, if happily they may feel after him or find him, although he be not far from every one of us: For in him we live, and move, and are.

Do you ever remember an evening when the deadening sounds of the world faded away, and you found yourself gazing down a new avenue of spiritual yearning? That was the voice of God. That was an actual grace. Did you ever feel a remorse, a sense of emptiness, a disgust with excesses, or wish for inner peace? That was the voice of God.

Make this experiment whether you believe in God or not. At your first opportunity stop in a Catholic Church for a visit. You need not believe as we Catholics do, that Our Lord is really and truly present in the tabernacle. But just sit there for an hour, and within that Hour you will experience a surpassing peace the like of which you never before enjoyed in your life.

You will ask yourself as a sensationalist once asked me when we made an all-night vigil of adoration in the Basilica of Sacre Coeur in Paris: "What is it that is in that Church?" Without voice or argument or thundering demands, you will have an awareness of something before which your spirit trembles — a sense of the Divine.

God walks into your soul with silent step. God comes to you, more than you go to Him. Every time a channel is made for Him, He pours into it His fresh gift of grace. And it is all done so undramatically — in prayer, in the sacraments, before the altar, in loving service of fellowman.

Never will His coming be what you expect, and yet never will it disappoint. The more you respond to His gentle pressure, the greater will be your freedom.

Too long have you wanted to be "just yourself." Can't you think of anything better than that? How about living as a Child of God?

THE SEVENTH WORD
- The Thinkers -

THE GREATEST PROBLEM of life is life itself. Remember how it puzzled Hamlet. What was the end of life? Would he want to continue to exist or not? When he died, would that be the end of him? Or would he go on living as in a dream? If there were nothing beyond this life, then well we might take it with a dagger, said Hamlet. If there is a life beyond, then we must worry about our conscience. Hamlet was very uncertain:

"To be, or not to be: that is the question.
Whether 'tis nobler in the mind to suffer
The slings and arrows of outrageous fortune
Or to take arms against a sea of troubles,
And, by opposing, end them? To die, to sleep
No more . . . 'Tis a consummation
Devoutly to be wished. To die, to sleep.

To sleep, perchance to dream; ay, there's
the rub!
For in that sleep of death what dreams
may come
When we have shuffled off this mortal
coil,
Must give us pause. There's the respect
That makes calamity of so long life.
For who would bear the whips and scorns
of time,
Th' oppressor's wrong, the proud man's
contumely,
The pangs of despised love, the law's
delay,
The insolence of office, and the spurns
That patient merit of th' unworthy takes,
When he himself might his quietus make
With a bare bodkin? Who would these
fardels bear,
To grunt and sweat under a weary life,
But that the dread of something after
death,
The undiscovered country from whose
bourn
No traveler returns, puzzles the will,
And makes us rather bear those ills we
have
Than fly to others that we know not of?

Thus conscience does make cowards of us all."

William Shakespeare

Now, turn from Hamlet's uncertainty of life to the Seventh Word that came from the Cross in loud, clear tones when there was a rupture of the heart through a rapture of love, as Christ bowed His Head and died: "Father, into Thy hands I commend my Spirit."

No doubt here; no problem here as to whether it's a sleep or a dream, or whether one should make his exit from the world with a dagger. Here was absolute certainty about the issue of life. Life is a return to the God Who made us. We came from God. To God again we go.

The Greeks had a theory that the perfect movement was the circular movement because the beginning was the end; and in a certain sense, that was right.

The beginning of our life which was God is also the end. We came from His creative Hands, and then, like a planet, when we have completed life's orbit, we go back to Him Who sent us on our way.

Life is like the coals, which in the prehistoric past as trees and foliage sucked in the fire and light of the sun, kept them hidden for years in the bowels of the earth, but finally when placed in the hearth give back to the sun that which they took from it.

And now the Son of God, like the Prodigal Son, goes back to the Father's House. For thirty-three years He has been in the foreign country of this earth, 'wasting His substance' among us, spending now even His last drop of blood. "And now glorify thou Me, O father, with thyself, with the glory which I had, before the world was, with thee" *(John 17:5).* "I have glorified thee on earth; I have finished the work which thou gavest me to do" *(John 17:4).* Now He could return home. "Father, into thy hands I commend my spirit."

Among those who gathered around the Cross was a centurion, so called because he commanded about 100 men, and who had duties similar to the sergeant of our army. The Gospel generally speaks well of centurions. As a soldier, he was often brought into contact with death.

On this particular occasion, He had nailed Our Lord to the Cross, then sat down, shook dice for His garments and watched Him die. But there was something peculiar about that Figure on the Central Cross.

Often the tongues of those crucified had to be cut out to prevent their blasphemies. But here was one Who forgave those who sent Him to His Death. Then too he noted that as the end grew near, He seemed to be getting stronger as if Death were not coming to meet Him, but He was going out to meet it. He was not dying on this Cross as other men died in bed.

The very second of death, He spoke in a loud, clear voice as if men were not taking away His life, but He was laying it down of Himself: "Father, into thy hands I commend my Spirit." These were not words of death, but of life. While He was accommodating Himself to death, it was only a milestone on the roadway in the onward march of life.

It made the sergeant think! Are we just animals who eat and sleep and then lie down to die and rot, or is there something after death, a God into Whose Hands we go to render an account of our stewardship. He shook off the thought for a moment but was rekindled to it when the earth shook, and the dead rose from their graves and walked.

He went on thinking about life and death as he broke the legs of the two thieves, for they were not yet dead. Coming to the Central Cross and finding Christ dead, He ran a spear into His Side. Blood and water came out; the Divine

Miser had hoarded up a few drops, to prove that Death is not the end of life.

These drops trickled down the spear, touched the centurion's hand, and tradition has it that he was immediately cured of a life-long affliction. In any case, he glorified God by saying: "Indeed this was the Son of God" *(Matthew 27: 54) (Luke 23:47) (Mark 15:39)*.

A soldier had found faith on a battlefield; a thinker discovered the answer to life's riddle in the midst of death. This life is not the end of all. That soldier became the representative of that seventh and last type who come in contact with the Cross, namely, the thinkers.

The term here is used in contradistinction to the intelligentsia, who *think* they are educated. By the thinkers is here understood all who concern themselves with the ultimate of life: why was I born, why am I here and whither am I going?

The thinkers do not necessarily mean the educated, nor even those who spend their life in meditation. But rather those who, once they are brought in contact with the spectacle of death, think the whole problem through.

One wonders what John thought when he saw that lance go into the side of his Lord. I wonder if he remembered that incident of the night before when Peter used a sword too, to cut off the ear of the servant of the High Priest.

I wonder too if John recalled what the Saviour answered to Peter: "Put up again thy sword into its place: for all that take the sword shall perish with the sword" *(Matthew 26:52)*.

Why then did not this sergeant perish with his sword? Because Our Lord seemed to suggest that it is all right if you use the sword against Me, but do not use it against your neighbor. That is why our Lord said to the soldiers: "I have told you that I am He. If therefore you seek Me, let these go their way" *(John 18:8)*.

There was a woman there along with John — the Mother of James and John whom Our Lord called 'sons of thunder.' Now there is thunder. The whole earth is trembling! And only one 'son of thunder' is there. Where is James? Why is he not there?

I wonder if she remembers, that good mother, the day that she went to Our Lord and said to Him: "Say that these my two sons, may sit, the one on thy right hand, and the other on thy left, in thy kingdom" (Matthew 20:21).

Mothers are always doing that. They are always maneuvering for their boys to get them into the right place. And the mother of these boys was no exception. She wanted to be sure that they would be in the upper classes.

And what did He say: "You know not what you ask. Can you drink the chalice that I shall drink?" *(Matthew 20:22)*. Only one of them could! Ah! The Kingdom of God is so different from the kingdom of men.

Mary Magdalen was there too. Poor Mary! Wherever there is ointment being poured forth, Mary will be there, and this time it is He Who pours out the crimson ointment of salvation. She saw it on the ground, and she suspected some of it was on her beautiful hair. As she once broke a vessel and gave everything in Simon's house, she now sees that Our Blessed Lord has done the same thing. He broke a vessel too when He gave all; and the odor filled the house: 'The House of the World!'

Then there was Mary, His Mother. It is peculiar about mothers that their children never grow up; even when they die, they still seem like children. Her mind goes back to a night long ago, when War began — the war against evil. She can recall so well looking out through the cracks in a stable roof and seeing a great star in the background of angels' wings, blazing in the night. To her it looked as if the Heavenly Father had hung out His Service Flag: His Son had gone to war!

Ye Mothers of the world, think ye not that she knows what it means to have a boy go to war! She remembers so well the night that He went out to battle, armed only in the flesh of man. And then the Battle came! This is not Bethlehem, Mary! This is Calvary! This is war! And unlike all the mothers of the world, you are in it. A queer war in which even mothers march upon the field! And you were wounded: pierced by seven swords! Everywhere the smell of death: nails, hammers, wounds, ghastly sights!

Mary — look up from the battlefield as thou didst look up from the crib. It is still dark! Dark in mid-afternoon. The sun has dimmed its light! It seems so far away! It looks exactly like a star! Remember the White Star of Christmas? Well — this is different! Mary! You are the first Gold Star Mother of the World!

ACKNOWLEDGMENTS

To the members of the Archbishop Fulton John Sheen Foundation in Peoria, Illinois. In particular, to the Most Rev. Daniel R. Jenky, C.S.C., Bishop of Peoria, for your leadership and fidelity to the cause of Sheen's canonization and the creation of this book.

www.archbishopsheencause.org

To the staff at Sophia Institute Press for their invaluable assistance in sharing the writings of Archbishop Fulton J. Sheen to a new generation of readers.

www.sophiainstitute.com

To the volunteers at the Archbishop Fulton J. Sheen Mission Society of Canada: your motto "Unless Souls are Saved, Nothing is Saved", speaks to the reality that Jesus Christ came into the world to make salvation available to all souls.

www.archbishopfultonjsheenmissionsocietyofcanada.org

To the good folks at 'Bishop Sheen Today'. We value your guidance, support, and prayers in helping us to share the wisdom of Archbishop Fulton J. Sheen. Your apostolic work of sharing his audio and video presentations along with his many writings to a worldwide audience is very much appreciated.

www.bishopsheentoday.com

And lastly, to Archbishop Fulton J. Sheen, whose teachings on Our Lord's Passion and His Seven Last Words continue to inspire me to love God more and to appreciate the gift of the Church. May we be so blessed as to imitate Archbishop Sheen's love for the saints, the sacraments, the Eucharist, and the Blessed Virgin Mary. May the Good Lord grant him a very high place in heaven!

ABOUT THE AUTHOR
Fulton J. Sheen
(1895–1979)

Archbishop Sheen, best known for his popularly televised and syndicated television program, Life is Worth Living, is held today as one of Catholicism's most widely recognized figures of the twentieth century.

Fulton John Sheen, born May 8, 1895, in El Paso, Illinois was raised and educated in the Roman Catholic faith. Originally named Peter John Sheen, he came to be known as a young boy by his mother's maiden name, Fulton. He was ordained a priest of the Diocese of Peoria at St. Mary's Cathedral in Peoria, IL on September 20, 1919.

Following his ordination, Sheen studied at the Catholic University of Louvain, where he earned a doctorate in philosophy in 1923. That same year, he received the Cardinal Mercier Prize for International Philosophy, becoming the first-ever American to earn this distinction.

Upon returning to America, after varied and extensive work throughout Europe, Sheen continued to preach and teach theology and philosophy from 1927 to 1950, at the Catholic University of America in Washington DC.

Beginning in 1930, Sheen hosted a weekly Sunday night radio broadcast called 'The Catholic Hour'. This broadcast captured many devoted listeners, reportedly drawing an audience of four million people every week for over twenty years.

In 1950, he became the National Director of the Society for the Propagation of the Faith, raising funds to support missionaries. During the sixteen years that he held this position, millions of dollars were raised to support the missionary activity of the Church. These efforts influenced tens of millions of people all over the world, bringing them to know Christ and his Church. In addition, his preaching and personal example brought about many converts to Catholicism.

In 1951, Sheen was appointed Auxiliary Bishop of the Archdiocese of New York. That same year, he began hosting his television program 'Life is Worth Living', which lasted for six years.

In the course of its run, that program competed for airtime with popular television programs hosted by the likes of Frank Sinatra and Milton Berle. Sheen's program held its own, and in 1953, just two years after its debut, he won an Emmy Award for "Most Outstanding Television Personality." Fulton Sheen credited the Gospel writers - Matthew, Mark, Luke, and John - for their valuable contribution to his success. Sheen's television show ran until 1957, boasting as many as thirty million weekly viewers.

In the Fall of 1966, Sheen was appointed Bishop of Rochester, New York. During that time, Bishop Sheen hosted another television series, 'The Fulton Sheen Program' which ran from 1961 to 1968, closely modeling the format of his 'Life is Worth Living' series.

After nearly three years as Bishop of Rochester, Fulton Sheen resigned and was soon appointed by Pope Paul VI as Titular Archbishop of the See of Newport, Wales. This new appointment allowed Sheen the flexibility to continue preaching.

Another claim to fame was Bishop Sheen's annual Good Friday homilies, which he preached for fifty-eight consecutive years at St. Patrick's Cathedral in New York City, and elsewhere. Sheen also led numerous retreats for priests and religious, preaching at conferences all over the world.

When asked by Pope St. Pius XII how many converts he had made, Sheen responded,

"Your Holiness, I have never counted them. I am always afraid that if I did count them, I might think I made them, instead of the Lord."

Sheen was known for being approachable and down to earth. He used to say, "If you want people to stay as they are, tell them what they want to hear. If you want to improve them, tell them what they should know." This he did, not only in his preaching but also through his numerous books and articles. His book titled 'Peace of Soul' was sixth on the New York Times best-seller list.

Three of Sheen's great loves were: the missions and the propagation of the faith; the Holy Mother of God and the Eucharist.

He made a daily holy hour of prayer before the Blessed Sacrament. It was from Jesus Himself that he drew strength and inspiration to preach the gospel, and in the Presence of Whom that he prepared his homilies. "I beg [Christ] every day to keep me strong physically and alert mentally, in order to preach His gospel and proclaim His Cross and Resurrection," he said. "I am so happy doing this that I sometimes feel that when I come to the good Lord in Heaven, I will take a few days' rest and then ask Him to allow me to come back again to this earth to do some more work."

His contributions to the Catholic Church are numerous and varied, ranging from educating in classrooms, churches, and homes, to preaching over a nationally-publicized radio show, and two television programs, as well as penning over sixty written works. Archbishop Fulton J. Sheen had a gift for communicating the Word of God in the most pure, simple way. His strong background in philosophy helped him to relate to everyone in a highly personalized manner. His timeless messages continue to have great relevance today. His goal was to inspire everyone to live a God-centered life with the joy and love that God intended.

On October 2, 1979, Archbishop Sheen received his greatest accolade, when Pope St. John Paul II embraced him at St. Patrick's Cathedral in New York City. The Holy Father said to him, "You have written and spoken well of the Lord Jesus. You are a loyal son of the Church."

The good Lord called Fulton Sheen home on December 9, 1979. His television broadcasts now available through various media, and his books, extend his earthly work of winning souls for Christ. Sheen's cause for canonization was opened in 2002. In 2012, Pope Benedict XVI declared him 'Venerable', and in July of 2019, Pope Francis formally approved the miracle necessary for Sheen's beatification and canonization process to move forward. The time and date for the church to declare Archbishop Fulton J. Sheen a saint is in God's hands.

J.M.J

Books Available Through Bishop Sheen Today Publishing

The Seven Last Words

Calvary and the Mass

The Holy Hour Prayer Book

The Cross and the Beatitudes

The Cross and the Crisis

Missions and the World Crisis

The Seven Last Words of Christ Explained

Father, Forgive Them for They Know Not What They Do.

This Day Thou Shall Be with Me in Paradise

Woman Behold Your Son; Behold Your Mother

My God! My God! Why Hast Thou Forsaken Me?

I Thirst

It is Finished

Father Into Your Hands I Commend My Spirit

Love One Another

The Divine Verdict

God Love You

The Seven Last Words Explained

The Priest Is Not His Own

The Cross and the Crib

Philosophies at War

Seven Words to the Cross

Seven Pillars of Peace

Love One Another

Seven Words of Jesus & Mary

Victory Over Vice

The Seven Virtues

For God and Country

God and War

Liberty, Equality and Fraternity

The Rainbow of Sorrow

www.bishopsheentoday.com

www.ingramcontent.com/pod-product-compliance
Lightning Source LLC
Chambersburg PA
CBHW021653120626
46545CB00002B/835